FERDINAND

The Engine that went off the Rails

Ann Benton

ISBN: 978-1-84550-444-1

Published by
Christian Focus Publications
Geanies House, Fearn, Ross-shire, IV20 1TW, Scotland, U.K.

www.christianfocus.com
email: info@christianfocus.com

Cover design by Daniel van Straaten
Illustrated by Michel de Boer
Printed and bound in China

If you would like a digital recording of this material
visit the Ferdinand page at www.christianfocus.com

ACKNOWLEDGEMENTS AND DEDICATION

Ferdinand was born out of a desire to illustrate truths embodied in a song. The song was written to help children learn a catechism. I want to express my indebtedness to Philip Wells, pastor of Calvary Church, Brighton, who first put the catechism to a traditional folk tune and to Bill Bygroves, pastor of Garston Bridge Chapel, Liverpool, who wrote additional verses.

It was while teaching this song to our own children at our breakfast table family prayers, that I hit on the idea of using my son's plastic clockwork train to teach the concepts of fall, ruin, rescue, justification and regeneration. The story was invented episode by episode, day by day, in an ad hoc way, until it took on a life of its own in our children's imaginations. Then I wrote it down.

My particular thanks must also go to our good friend, Mike Parsons, for his painstaking work on the original soundtrack. The children who sang on that soundtrack are now grown up with children of their own. And it is to one member of that next generation, our grandson Freddie, that I dedicate this book with the prayer that these truths may be as precious to him as the story is enjoyable.

Ann Benton
Guildford
January 2009

The Inventor's Best Invention

Once upon a time there was a very, very clever Inventor who made a beautiful railway engine. It was brightly coloured and shiny. It was a steam engine and it was the best thing that the Inventor had ever invented, and he had invented many wonderful things.

He had made the track on which his trains ran. It went through tunnels and over bridges, up hills and down valleys. It had many stations and the engine could draw trucks and carry cargo back and forth between them.

This railway engine was so special, it even had a name. It was called Ferdinand. Everybody who saw it, and who knew the Inventor, would say as they saw it pass, 'You can tell the Inventor made that engine. Isn't it beautifully made? What craftsmanship! What lovely design!'

Ferdinand was made to run on those two rails on that track. Sometimes as he steamed along, he would look with fascination at the green fields full of daisies or the cool, rushing streams. But if ever he tried to get off his track, he would get himself into terrible, terrible trouble, because railway engines are made to run on rails.

While Ferdinand did what he was made to do, taking things from station to station for the Inventor, he was happy and all was well. The Inventor watched him from the window of his inventing house and was pleased with what he had made.

SONG
Who made you? God made me.
What else did God make? God made all things.
Why did God make all things? For His own glory.

APPLICATION
As Ferdinand ran on the two rails so God made us to live according
to his two great commands, to love him with all our
heart and to love other people as ourselves.

SCRIPTURE VERSE
Genesis 1:1

The Very Helpful Book

Although the Inventor kept a close watch on Ferdinand, Ferdinand never saw the Inventor. The Inventor had a great deal to do in his inventing house, keeping everything going. But Ferdinand had a very good friend, who had been sent by the Inventor to take care of him. This friend had been in the army and was always known as the Captain. He had a horse called Roscoe, whom he rode alongside Ferdinand's track.

When the Inventor had asked the Captain to come and look after Ferdinand, he had given him a large book. On the front of it were the words 'Manual for Operating Railway Engines'.

However, the Captain thought it looked rather boring so he never read it. But one day Ferdinand broke down. He slowed down and then he just stopped. The Captain was very worried. He was not clever like the Inventor. He did not understand how to get a railway engine to go.

He cautiously took a look at the boiler and at the pistons. He could not see what was wrong. All this time Roscoe kept nudging him with his nose.

'Don't bother me now, Roscoe. There's a good chap. I'm trying to sort this engine out.'

But Roscoe kept on fidgeting and nudging until finally the Captain gave him some attention.

'What is it then?' he started to say, when he saw underneath Roscoe's foot the book, the Manual for Operating Railway Engines.

'Aha!' he said. 'Absolutely! Absolutely! Old chap.'

Then he looked at the book and didn't say anything for a very long time. Every now and then he looked inside Ferdinand and grunted. Finally, he said, 'I've got it!' and he set to work.

When the engine got up steam and the wheels began to turn again, Roscoe leapt around for joy. All the Captain would say was, 'It's in that book. It's absolutely amazing! It's all in the book!'

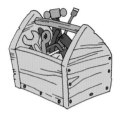

SONG
Where do we learn about God?
In the Bible book.
Who wrote that?
Holy people taught by God.
What do we learn there?
To love Him and obey.

APPLICATION
God has given us a book which tells us how best to run our lives.
That book is the Bible.

SCRIPTURE VERSE
2 Timothy 3:16

More About The Inventor

After the time Ferdinand broke down, the Captain was never far from his book. He sometimes read bits of it out loud to Ferdinand because as well as having a lot in it about Ferdinand, it had a great amount to say about the Inventor.

Ferdinand had begun to be very curious about the Inventor. He knew where the Inventor lived, but there were no rails to the Inventor's door. The Captain said that the Inventor had a very, very special engine in his workshop, but Ferdinand had never seen it and he wasn't sure whether to believe the Captain about that.

The Captain also said that the Inventor did quite often come out of his house sometimes to drive his special engine along the track, and sometimes to walk beside the track, but Ferdinand never caught a glimpse of him.

One day Ferdinand saw alongside his track the footprints of some very large boots. He was frightened, but very excited when the Captain said he thought they were the Inventor's. Very cautiously Ferdinand moved along the track following the footprints. At a bend in the track Ferdinand stopped.

There were two reasons for this. Firstly, he was rather nervous, not knowing if he dared to come near to the Inventor who was such a special person. The other reason was that he had run out of steam. In his excitement about the footprints, he had forgotten to fill up with water.

The Captain and Roscoe managed to nose Ferdinand around the corner. There they saw the footprints which suddenly turned across the fields where Ferdinand could not go. But more wonderful, there at the side of the track was an enormous trough of water which neither Ferdinand nor the Captain remembered ever having seen before. As he filled his boiler, Ferdinand was excited and puzzled all at once. But how did he know? And why did he...? The Captain grinned and nodded, tapping his book.

The Inventor's a very special person, so good and so clever. Ferdinand sighed. There are some things a railway engine can't understand. Then with a great toot, he steamed down the track. 'But I'm very glad, I'm very glad!, I'm very glad!' he shouted all the way.

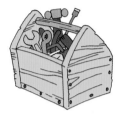

SONG
What is God like? God is great.
God is good. God is holy.
God is all-powerful. God is love.

APPLICATION
God is far greater than we can understand. He is also very, very good.
He deserves our worship and our praise.

SCRIPTURE VERSE
Exodus 15:11-13

Ferdinand Goes Off The Rails

There was only one thing that Ferdinand was not allowed to do. He was not allowed to go off the track. It was all very simple. He just had to stay on the rails. Ferdinand's favourite piece of track ran along the top of a cliff by the coast. He loved to look at the blue sea and the waves. How he wished he could go to the seashore.

Now, the Inventor had an enemy whose name was Sunny Jim. Sunny Jim had a big cheerful grin, but he wasn't as friendly as he looked. It was his aim in life to spoil everything that the Inventor had made. Sunny Jim used to sit at the top of the cliff and ask Ferdinand as he passed by if he would like a day at the seaside. 'Just what you need!' said Sunny Jim. 'You're working too hard!'

One day Ferdinand came around the track and saw that Sunny Jim had been busy.

'Branch line to the seaside this way!' shouted Sunny Jim, pointing down a side track he had made.

'You need a break!' called Sunny Jim and he laughed heartily as he said that.

Ferdinand knew that this was not the Inventor's way. He could hear the Captain and Roscoe riding up behind him, calling, 'Stop! I say – stop!'

But Ferdinand was really only listening to Sunny Jim and to the sound of the waves on the seashore. Ferdinand took the branch line to the seaside. He did not see that the line went straight to the edge of the cliff until he was falling down and down and finally landed on the rocky seashore. The Captain was looking down from the top of the cliff. Very faintly Ferdinand could hear his desperate cry, 'How could you break the rule? I can't get you up! Wait! The Inventor's coming round the track in a train. He's stopping. Oh Ferdinand, old friend, you're in dreadful trouble!'

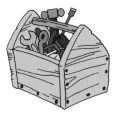

SONG

What is sin? Transgression of the law.
What does that mean?
Doing the things that God forbids.
What does every sin deserve?
God's angry punishment.

APPLICATION

Ferdinand disobeyed the Inventor and from the first man, Adam,
onwards we have all disobeyed God.

SCRIPTURE VERSE

1 John 3:4

Ferdinand in Trouble

Ferdinand looked around him. He was on the seashore. Yes, Sunny Jim had been right about that, but it was more like a scrapyard. All around Ferdinand, scattered amongst the rocks and pebbles of the seashore were battered, rusty and broken parts of railway engines. Somehow Sunny Jim was already there on the beach, laughing delightedly and leaping about with a big hammer in his hand. He was smashing things up and enjoying every minute. Ferdinand was horrified and very, very frightened, but there was nothing he could do. Now he was off the rails, he couldn't move. 'I'm going to be broken up,' he said painfully.

'That's right,' said Sunny Jim grinning, 'I told you, you needed a break!'

Ferdinand knew it was all his own fault. What would the Inventor say? Ferdinand dared not think.

He heard the Captain again, 'Ferdinand! Look up!' Ferdinand could not look up. He could not move. All he saw was Sunny Jim. He did not see the lowering of a great iron hook on the end of a strong iron chain, which was attached to a beautiful golden engine on the rails at the top of the cliff. Ferdinand did not know and would not have guessed that although he did not deserve it at all, the Inventor was organising a rescue.

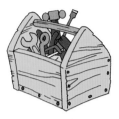

SONG
What is grace?
The free gift of God.
We receive
Forgiveness that we don't deserve.
How does God show His grace?
By giving us His Son.

APPLICATION
God is so great and marvellous in His love that even though we have disobeyed Him on purpose many times and didn't care that we had, yet He has made a way to rescue us.

SCRIPTURE VERSE
Ephesians 2:4

Ferdinand Tries To Escape

Roscoe and the Captain peered over the top of the cliff. They tried to encourage Ferdinand as they watched the rescue operation, for it was not they who were attempting to save poor Ferdinand. The work was going to be done by the shining gold engine on the rails. Its name was printed in huge letters on its side – Morning Star. In the cab was the Inventor. He was giving all his attention to directing the rescue.

While Morning Star was getting up steam to haul up Ferdinand, and the Captain was guiding the great chain and hook towards Ferdinand's fender, Ferdinand himself had decided to make an effort to escape Sunny Jim's hammer.

'If I could just get my own fire going again,' he thought, 'I've water and I've coal, I'll get away!' So he hissed and strained, he gasped and struggled, but despite all his efforts, he could not fan a single spark into a flame.

Sunny Jim found Ferdinand's efforts very amusing. However, the sight of the Inventor's hook and chain wiped the smile off his face. He was furious! He started grabbing pieces of loose rock from the beach and he hurled them first at Ferdinand, then at the chain and then with incredible strength, up over the top of the cliff at Morning Star.

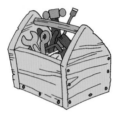

SONG
Salvation,
What is it about?
Being saved from sin
Freely by the grace of God;
Not by works which we have done
So nobody can boast.

APPLICATION
People often imagine that they can save themselves. But that is impossible.
Only God can save.

SCRIPTURE VERSE
Colossians 1:13

Ferdinand is Rescued

Ferdinand felt the great hook grip his fender. He also felt the bangs and scratches of the rocks that Sunny Jim was throwing. It was terrible! The Captain was shouting something: 'Hurry! Hurry! There's no time to be lost! Ferdinand, tip out your coal! Let your water out!'

'But then I'll never get away!' moaned Ferdinand, feeling the strain as Morning Star began to pull.

Ferdinand knew he had to do what the Captain said. He knew somehow that his rescue depended on it. So he emptied out his water and his coal. Immediately, being so much lighter he was swinging on the end of the chain up the cliff face. He was very frightened. Supposing the chain should break? But he was encouraged when the Captain shouted, 'Don't worry! The Inventor's in control.'

It seemed ages, but in fact it was quite soon that Ferdinand found himself being dragged along the grass on the cliff top. The rocks were still being thrown, but when Ferdinand caught sight of Morning Star steaming along the track with such strength, he was thrilled! Roscoe and the Captain helped get Ferdinand back on the rails. 'Now, all you have to do is follow Morning Star,' they said.

Ferdinand would have followed that engine anywhere, but he realised he had no fire in his furnace, no water and no coal. 'I can't!' he said, 'I'm useless!'

Then he realised that his wheels were turning. He was following Morning Star. He had already moved some way along the track before he realised the reason. That same hook and chain which had first linked him to Morning Star was still very much attached to his fender. He was following. He could not do anything else.

SONG
What must I do to be saved?
I must repent.
What does that mean?
To hate and forsake my sin.
What else must I do?
Have faith in Jesus Christ.

What is faith?
Faith is trusting Christ.
We believe everything that God has said.
How do we come to faith?
God's Spirit works in us.

APPLICATION
To be saved, to become a Christian, you have to empty yourself
and trust only in the Lord Jesus Christ.

SCRIPTURE VERSES
Mark 1:15; John 20:28

The Great Explosion

As Ferdinand rolled along the track, he kept watching Morning Star ahead of him. Sunny Jim was now leaping alongside the track shouting and hurling bigger and bigger rocks. Ferdinand tried not to listen to the awful things that he was saying.

Nothing seemed able to stop the steady forward progress of Morning Star until that is, he slowed down to a halt near the Inventor's house on a brand new siding which led into the engine shed and workshop. Sunny Jim saw his opportunity. As Morning Star stopped, Sunny Jim's huge hands gripped the back of Ferdinand. Sunny Jim pulled Ferdinand from the back. Morning Star would not let go and tugged from the front.

For a dreadful moment, Ferdinand feared he would burst, but the tug of war suddenly ended. There was an enormous explosion! Strange to say, the force of it shot Ferdinand safely into the engine shed, but he saw Morning Star leave the track and hurtle straight through the wall at the back of the shed.

It was as if after the effort of the rescue, Morning Star had given his all. He could do no more. In that final struggle his boiler had burst and his engine exploded. 'He was only a railway engine after all,' thought Ferdinand sadly.

Then the Inventor appeared and closed the doors of the shed behind Ferdinand. It was then that Ferdinand realised that Sunny Jim was no longer gripping his rear. Ferdinand cried tears of relief. He was safe from Sunny Jim, but what had he done to Morning Star?

He gazed at the hole in the back of the engine shed. In the strange explosion somehow Morning Star had crashed sideways through the back of the shed, leaving a hole which was the size and shape of Morning Star. In horror Ferdinand stared through the hole. Outside on the grass a delighted Sunny Jim, with an enormous wheelbarrow, was gathering up the fragments of the beautiful golden engine that had been Morning Star.

SONG
Who is Christ? God's own Son.
Did He ever sin?
No, He fully kept the law.
Why did He die then?
To take our sins away.

APPLICATION
In order to save us, the Lord Jesus Christ had to give His life.
He died for our sins.

SCRIPTURE VERSE
John 3:16; 1 Peter 3:18

Sunny Jim's Triumph

While Ferdinand was safe in the Inventor's workshop, Sunny Jim, as pleased as could be, ran off with his wheelbarrow over the fields to the cliff top. It was night when he arrived there and with a great heave he tipped the golden pieces over the edge of the cliff into his scrapyard.

'I've won!' he shouted. 'I've won! I've won! I went after Ferdinand, but I got the best engine of all in his place' and at this Sunny Jim held his sides and laughed.

He did not know that someone was watching him. Someone in very large boots. He did not know that this person then went back to his workshop and looked at a ruined engine with hardly a working part and that as he did so, he was pleased that Ferdinand was safe.

Ferdinand himself, when he awoke early next morning, still gazed in horror at the Morning Star-shaped hole in the back of the engine shed. He asked the Captain what had happened and when he heard, he felt really awful.

'I should have been in that scrapyard,' he said, 'And now Morning Star has been broken up instead of me and it's all my fault.'

But as the sun rose it seemed to Ferdinand that the hole in the wall was not an empty space. It seemed as if a beautiful golden engine was actually taking shape in the hole.

'You mark my words, old friend!' said the Captain. 'We haven't seen the last of Morning Star.'

SONG
How did Jesus die?
He died upon the Cross.
Who nailed Him there?
Those who were God's enemies.
Though they meant evil
God planned it for our good.

APPLICATION
When the Lord Jesus Christ died on the Cross, Satan thought he had won.
But it was all just as God had planned for our rescue.
And three days later Jesus rose again from the dead.

SCRIPTURE VERSE
Acts 2:23, 24

The Inventor Gets to Work

Later that morning the Inventor came in. In one hand he carried an enormous box of tools. In the other hand he had some spare parts. He started very gently and methodically to take Ferdinand to pieces. The Captain sat on a bench, watching very closely while at the same time referring to his manual.

'According to this manual, dear chap,' he said to Ferdinand. 'You are going to have to be completely remade.'

Ferdinand looked very glum indeed. The Inventor said nothing. He was far too busy.

The Captain looked hard at the replacement parts. 'Surely those are parts of Morning Star,' he said. He had before him a large diagram in the manual.

'Aha! The perfect railway engine!' he said, 'And Morning Star was it. You won't go far wrong if you're like him, Ferdinand.'

The Inventor's head had disappeared inside Ferdinand where he was busy changing parts and cleaning up. It was some hours later that the Inventor packed up his tools and wiped his hands.

Ferdinand was a little disappointed. He had hoped he might get some shining new bodywork like Morning Star, but he knew that he had a fresh start inside. It was as if that awful incident about the cliff had never happened. He was determined to work really hard for the Inventor.

He saw the Inventor tear up all his old worksheets with all the mistakes. The Inventor put fresh instructions in the cab. The Captain filled Ferdinand's boiler and loaded up some coal. Then came the moment that Ferdinand had been waiting for.

The Inventor lit his fire, the steam built up and soon Ferdinand knew he was ready to go. With a great whistle of joy Ferdinand reversed out of the engine shed.

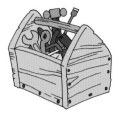

SONG
How can we have a new start?
By being born again.
What does that mean?
God's Spirit comes to live in us.
What does He do there?
He makes us more like Christ.

APPLICATION
When someone becomes a Christian, God the Holy Spirit comes to live in him
and makes a difference in the way he lives. Gradually that person is changed to become
more and more like Jesus.

SCRIPTURE VERSE
Titus 3:5

Back on the Track

Ferdinand was back on the track. The track had not changed at all and Ferdinand had a lot to do. It was his first day out and he wanted to do well. But just around the first corner, he met a familiar figure. It was Sunny Jim who gave Ferdinand a broad smile and waved.

'Glad to see you back, Ferdinand!' he called in a most friendly voice.

Ferdinand was very confused by this. At his first stop Ferdinand saw Sunny Jim again and this time he noticed something in Sunny Jim's hand. It was the end of what appeared to be a very long hosepipe. What was he up to?

Before Ferdinand could spend any more time staring and trying to work this out, something else happened. He heard a deep resonant toot ahead of him on the track. This made him look up and when he did, he forgot all about Sunny Jim for there at a nearby junction was Morning Star as gleaming and golden as ever!

'The Inventor must have made him again!' thought Ferdinand.

And this did not seem too wonderful a thing for the Inventor to have done. At once Ferdinand knew that Morning Star was reminding him to get on with his work. Gladly with an answering whistle, Ferdinand did so.

Ferdinand saw Morning Star many times that day, but Sunny Jim was also around every corner and always he had that hosepipe.

'May I top up your boiler for you?' he asked Ferdinand at one stop.

When Ferdinand hesitated, Sunny Jim made a leap for the cab. At that moment there was a warning toot from Morning Star. Ferdinand let off his brake and moved with such a jolt that Sunny Jim fell out of the cab! It was not a minute too soon. Sunny Jim had already opened the door of the furnace and had been about to put out Ferdinand's fire and that was what Sunny Jim tried to do again and again. Ferdinand had to be careful to keep his boiler good and hot and to have nothing to do with Sunny Jim. And he always kept a lookout for Morning Star who appeared on the track from time to time to warn or to guide.

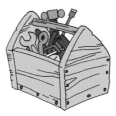

SONG
Where is Jesus now?
He's risen from the dead.
He's now in heaven
As our prophet, priest and king,
Sitting at the right hand
Of Majesty on high.

APPLICATION
It is not always easy to follow the Lord Jesus. God's enemy, Satan, is against us.
But Jesus has promised to help us and He can be trusted not to let us down.

SCRIPTURE VERSE
Hebrews 8:1

Ferdinand Has a Bad Day

Every day when his work was done Ferdinand had to report back to the Inventor. There was a new siding by that workshop where Ferdinand had been changed. Ferdinand would go there and wait outside that hole in the wall. The strange thing was, it wasn't a hole any more. It was filled with a coloured glass railway engine just like Morning Star. The Inventor had made it, and he would look through it at Ferdinand and wave him on if he was satisfied that all was well.

But one day Ferdinand got everything wrong. First of all he didn't read his instructions properly and he went in the wrong direction. When the Captain and Roscoe rode after him, he felt cross and started to get faster, blowing his whistle loudly so that he would not hear them.

He was so busy doing this, he forgot to look out for Sunny Jim who was waiting round the corner with handfuls of gravel which he threw into Ferdinand's face.

Scratched and blinded, Ferdinand knew better than to stop so he chugged on, not knowing where he was going. He did not see that Sunny Jim had built a wall across the track.

Suddenly Ferdinand went into the wall! His front was dented and crumpled. Sunny Jim ran to jump into the cab. Ferdinand heard the resonant toot of Morning Star. It aroused him just in time. He reversed, battered as he was, but he still had fire and steam and he went with all his might back down the track.

That evening when he reported back to the Inventor, he was ashamed and very sorry. He thought that the Inventor would see his scratches and dents and be angry, but when Ferdinand stopped by the Morning Star window the Inventor looked at him and smiled. Whatever the Inventor knew about Ferdinand and he knew everything, he did not seem to see the scratches and bumps. Morning Star covered them all.

SONG
Justified.
What is it?
Just as if
I had never sinned,
Receiving the righteousness
of Jesus Christ.

What is righteousness?
Being pure in the sight of God.
When God looks on us
He sees the holiness of Christ
Which we can only have
through Jesus Christ, God's Son.

APPLICATION
A Christian is not a perfect person. But a Christian knows that God is always his friend,
because Jesus died for sins. Because of what Jesus has done,
a Christian is welcome with God.

SCRIPTURE VERSE
Romans 3:25, 26.

Sunny Jim Tries Again

A part of Ferdinand's track still lay along that cliff top. It worried Ferdinand very much that one day he might do the same thing again. He might just take that branch line and not stop in time and go over the cliff. Surely then he would be lost forever.

One day it happened that Ferdinand got so frightened on the top of that cliff that he stopped on the track. He did not dare move whether forwards or backwards. The Captain and Roscoe found him there.

The Captain immediately looked into his manual. He tried to encourage Ferdinand, but he still could not get him to move. In the end the Captain sent Roscoe with a message for the Inventor.

Meanwhile Sunny Jim appeared. 'Well, well!' he cried, 'The Inventor is finished with you. You're only fit for my scrapyard after all!'

Speedily, Sunny Jim fetched a rope. Between the track and the edge of the cliff was a very tall, strong tree. Sunny Jim attached one end of the rope to Ferdinand. He tossed the other end through a fork in the branches of the tree and caught it at the other side. He was determined to show the Inventor that Ferdinand was really finished this time.

He started to pull at his end of the rope intending to hoist Ferdinand into the tree and then push him the other way down over the cliff into the scrapyard. He had tied his end of the rope around himself.

With amazing strength he began to haul.

Ferdinand's front wheels left the ground. The Captain was emptying his pockets looking for his pocket knife. Then around the corner came the Inventor on Roscoe.

The Inventor jumped from the horse into Ferdinand's cab, fired up the boiler and put the engine into reverse. The back wheels were still on the track. He started moving slowly at first then faster. Now it was Sunny Jim who was leaving the ground. The engine with the Inventor driving was too much for him. Dangling in the air he knew he was beaten.

The Captain finally found what he was looking for. He started sawing at the rope with his pocket knife. Having gone up almost to the fork in the tree suddenly Sunny Jim found himself falling very, very fast. He landed on the cliff top tied up in his own rope and before he could stop himself, he had bounced over the edge of the cliff into his own scrapyard.

By this time the Inventor had driven Ferdinand backwards some way down the track. Now he called to the engine, 'Don't worry, Ferdinand, I'll get you home' and Morning Star led the way in triumph.

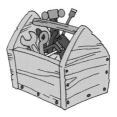

SONG
How do I know I'm saved?
God's Spirit works in me.
He tells me that
My sins are all forgiven.
He gives me then a certain hope
of happiness in heaven.

APPLICATION
Anyone who has repented and trusted in the Lord Jesus Christ may be sure of going
eventually to heaven. The Bible says so and God the Holy Spirit confirms it in our hearts
and by keeping us on the rails.

SCRIPTURE VERSE
Romans 10:9

Catechism in Song

Moderately

Trad. arr. J. Stephens

All verses except last   last verse

C

A: Introduction   B: Verses   C: Interlude (between verses)

Based on a traditional Cornish folk tune called 'Hal an Tow'.
Words by Philip Wells and Bill Bygroves.

CHRISTIAN FOCUS PUBLICATIONS

Christian Focus | Christian Heritage | CF4K | Mentor

Christian Focus Publications publishes books for adults and children under its four main imprints: Christian Focus, Christian Heritage, CF4K and Mentor. Our books reflect that God's word is reliable and Jesus is the way to know him, and live for ever with him.

Our children's publication list includes a Sunday school curriculum that covers pre-school to early teens; puzzle and activity books. We also publish personal and family devotional titles, biographies and inspirational stories that children will love.

If you are looking for quality Bible teaching for children then we have an excellent range of Bible story and age specific theological books.

From pre-school to teenage fiction, we have it covered!

Find us at our web page:
www.christianfocus.com

CF4·K
Because you're never too young to know Jesus